I CHOOSE
to Reduce, Reuse, Recycle

I CHOOSE SERIES

ELIZABETH ESTRADA

I CHOOSE
to Reduce, Reuse, Recycle

I
CHOOSE
SERIES

ELIZABETH ESTRADA

I never used to think about
The future of the **Earth**,
Or how I should appreciate
The planet of my **birth**.

The mountains and the valleys,
The rivers and the **sea** -
I took them all for granted.
Just as casual as could **be**.

I had heard about pollution -
That we're poisoning the **air**.
We're damaging the planet,
So we need to be **aware**.

In class, our teacher taught us
We each can make an **impact**.
We can save the world.
All we have to do is **act**.

Reduce, reuse, recycle is
An awesome way to **start**.
And it's down to each of us
To try and play a **part**.

Reduce means cutting back
On all the trash that we **create**.
The waste we have to bury
At a quite alarming **rate**.

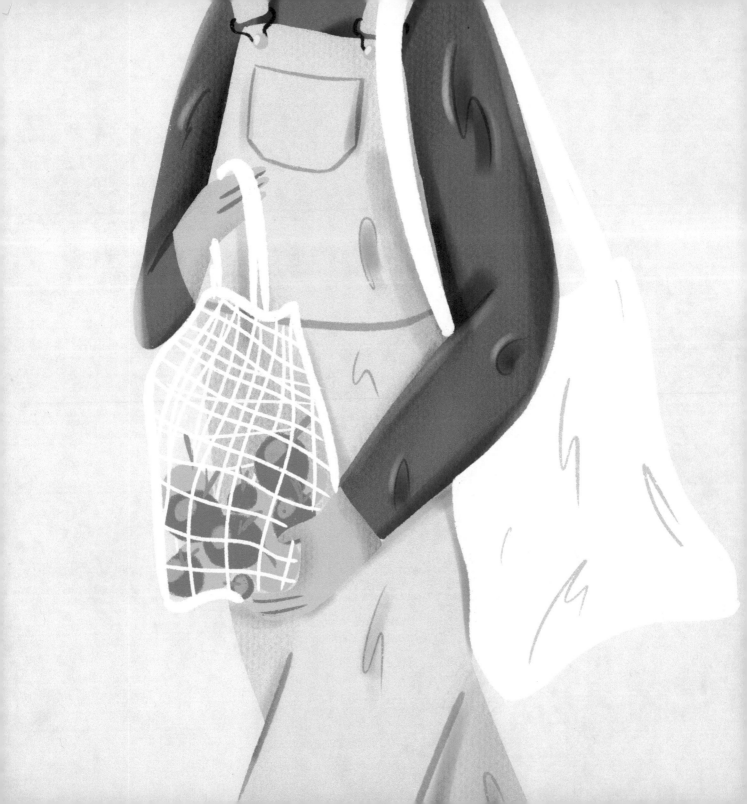

Reuse means taking used things
That is perfectly **okay**
And trying to make more use of it
In many different **ways**.

Recycle means you take the old
And make it something **new**
Like metal, plastic, wood, and glass.
That's just to name a **few**.

By saving our resources,
We can help keep our planet **clean**.
Reduce, reuse, recycle -
Simply follow that **routine**.

The night before I went to bed,
I made a little **list**
Of all the ways a kid like me
Is able to **assist**.

I want to switch the lights off
When there's no one in the **room**,
Reducing wasted energy
That every house **consumes**.

I want to brush my teeth each day
Without the faucets **on**
As running water is a waste.
And when it's gone, it's **gone**!

I can use a reusable box
For the lunch I take to **school**.
Throwing away bags everyday
Just isn't very **cool**.

I want to draw on paper
Using both sides of the **sheet**.
If I can save a tree or two,
That really would be **neat**.

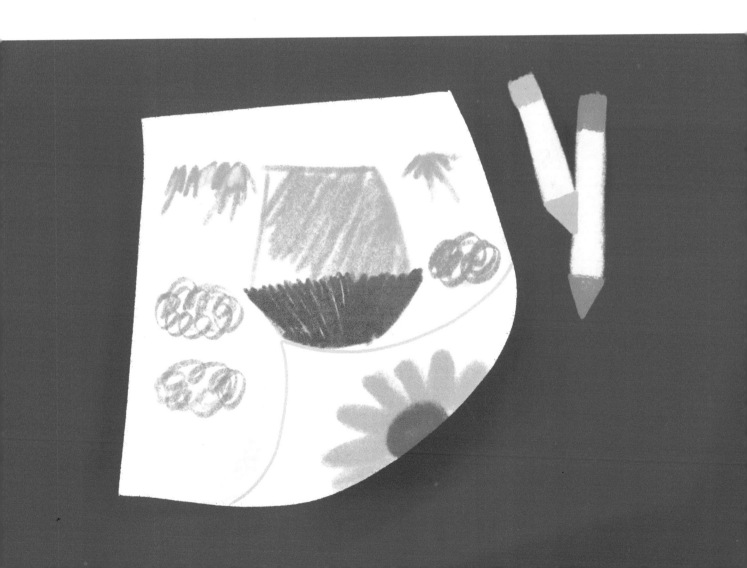

I want my toys to be reused
By children who have **none**.
Donating those I'm finished with,
So other kids can have **fun**.

I want to give a pile of clothes -
The ones that I've **outgrown**
To Goodwill stores and charities,
So they can find a **home**.

I want to give the books I've read
To libraries for **free**,
So other kids will have the chance
To read them just like **me**.

I want to save my leftovers
As food can be **ideal**
For storing in the freezer
To reuse for other **meals**.

I want to start recycling
All my bags, jars, and **cans**.
The bottles that I use
Are also in my **plans**.

I want to use the colored bins
To separate our **waste**,
So all of my recyclables
Can reach the proper **place**.

I want a healthy planet.
And I truly **understand**
That what happens to
The Earth is in my **hands**.

One person can make a difference
Because we each have an **impact**.
I choose to reduce, reuse, recycle.
So that our planet remains **intact**.

Ways I Can Save My Earth

1. TURN OFF LIGHTS WHEN YOU LEAVE THE ROOM. DURING THE DAY, OPEN YOUR CURTAINS AND ENJOY NATURAL LIGHT.

2. USE A REUSABLE WATER BOTTLE, AND STOP BUYING PLASTIC DISPOSABLE BOTTLES.

3. WHEN YOU CAN, WALK OR RIDE YOUR BIKE AND GET SOME EXERCISE! TRY TO KEEP A PHYSICAL DISTANCE OF TWO METERS FROM OTHER PEOPLE.

4. REUSE SCRAP PAPER FOR WRITING NOTES OR CREATING CRAFTS.

5. UNPLUG UNUSED CHARGERS.

6. RECYCLE CANS, BOTTLES, PAPER, BOOKS, AND EVEN TOYS.

7. TURN OFF THE WATER WHEN YOU'RE BRUSHING YOUR TEETH.

8. PUT YOUR COMPUTER TO "SLEEP" INSTEAD OF LEAVING IT ON WITH THE SCREENSAVER RUNNING.

9. KEEP YOUR SHOWERS SHORT TO CONSERVE WATER.

10. USE REUSABLE FOOD CONTAINERS FOR YOUR LUNCH.

11. CHOOSE RECHARGEABLE BATTERIES, THEN RECYCLE THEM WHEN THEY DIE.

12. BORROW A DIGITAL BOOK FROM THE LIBRARY — IT'S A GREAT WAY TO REDUCE WASTE.

13. STOP USING DISPOSABLE BAGS, USE REUSABLE BAGS.

14. TAKE SHORTER SHOWERS.

15. USE NON-TOXIC CLEANERS IN YOUR HOUSE AND EXPLAIN THAT THESE ARE BETTER FOR THE ENVIRONMENT.

16. CARPOOL AT LEAST ONCE A WEEK. IT'S FUN AND ENVIRONMENTALLY FRIENDLY!

17. VOLUNTEER FOR TREE PLANTING PROGRAMS OR CREEK CLEANUPS

18. PROPERLY RECYCLE OF USED BATTERIES.

19. START A COMPOST IN YOUR YARD.

20. PLANT A TREE TOGETHER AND LEARN ALL ABOUT THE MANY WAYS TREES BENEFIT OUR ENVIRONMENT.

21. BEFORE BUYING ANYTHING NEW, SEARCH FOR USED OR FREE ITEMS!

CPSIA information can be obtained
at www.ICGtesting.com
Printed in the USA
LVHW072055290921
699046LV00002B/27